NORTH AMERICAN INDIANS

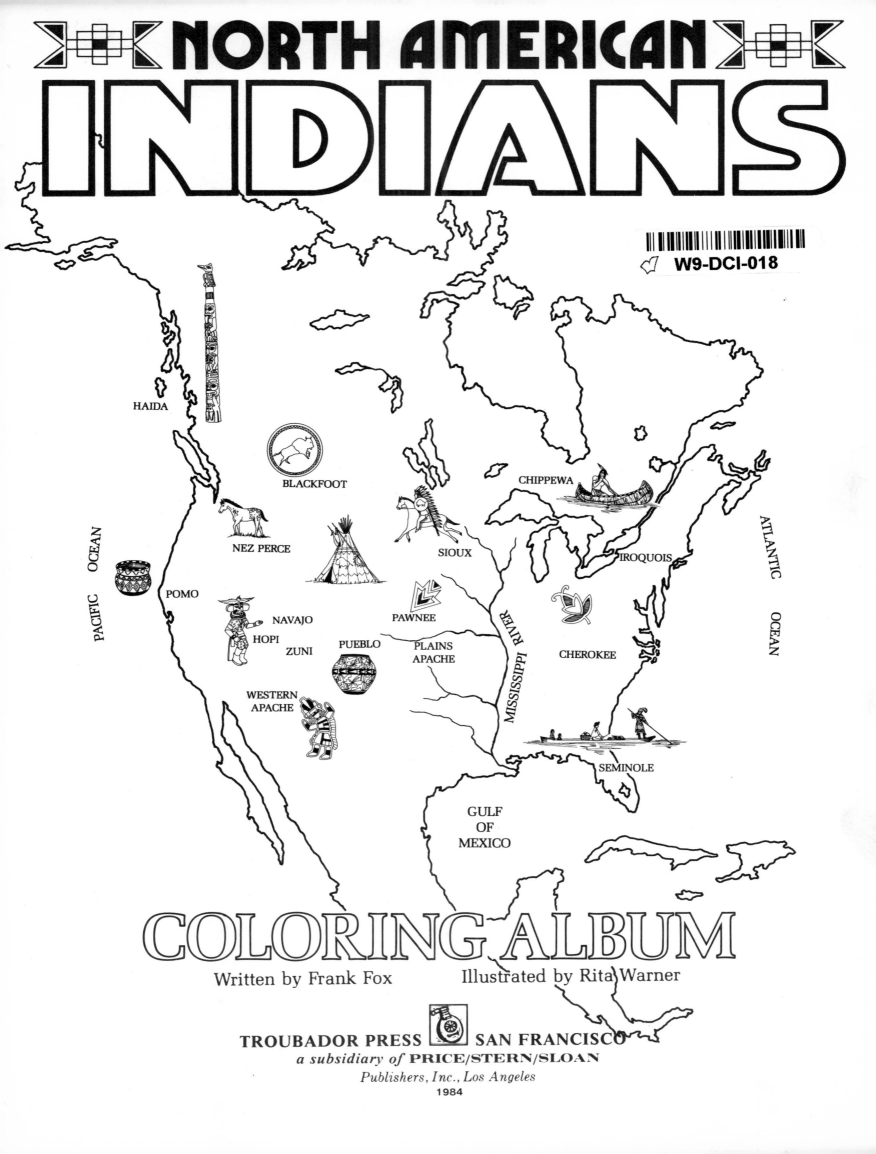

W9-DCI-018

COLORING ALBUM

Written by Frank Fox   Illustrated by Rita Warner

TROUBADOR PRESS ⊘ SAN FRANCISCO
a subsidiary of **PRICE/STERN/SLOAN**
Publishers, Inc., Los Angeles
1984

IROQUOIS

From their home in the forests of New York, a group of Indian tribes came to be known and feared throughout much of what was to become the Eastern United States and Southeastern Canada. The French called them "Iroquois." They called themselves *Hodenosaunee*, "The People of The Longhouse."

Several Iroquoian tribes lived on both sides of the Canadian border in an area vital to both English and French colonial interests. The most famous of these were the five tribes who originally created the League of The Iroquois—The Seneca, Cayuga, Onondaga, Oneida and Mohawk tribes.

Iroquois Indians lived an agricultural and hunting life. They inhabited stockaded villages around which the men had cleared the woods to make fields for planting. There the women raised many varieties of corn, beans and squash. They also gathered wild berries. The men took small game and deer as well as gathering in large amounts of fish in wide nets. Men traveled in war parties to raid the camps of other Indians and return with captives and glory.

Property and inheritance rights passed through the mother's side of a family. Thus the fields, crops and great longhouses, in which several families lived, belonged to the women. When a man married, he went to live with his wife's family.

The longhouse was an immense wooden structure of elm bark slabs on a pole frame with an arched roof. They were usually 15 to 35 meters long, and some may have been even larger. Inside, families lived in compartments separated by storage areas down both sides. Cooking fires were lit along the middle. Dogs also shared the longhouse. It was a lively place.

Iroquois did not invent wampum, but they employed it extensively. The light and dark wampum beads (often white and purple), were fashioned from pieces of shell, and placed on strings or formed into belts. The beads of wampum belts were arranged to preserve and express specific meanings. Certain Iroquois were skilled in "reading" the history, customs, ceremonies, laws and legends which were recorded in different wampum. Wampum belts were given to solemnify treaties, agreements and other important matters.

The system of tribal government of The League of The Iroquois is distinctive among North American Indians. When Dutch settlers arrived in New York in the early 1600's, they found the five Iroquois tribes organized into a league which these Indians called "The Great Peace." The league's council was composed of about 50 members, known as "sachems," who decided league policy and relations with outside tribes. Each of the five tribes controlled its own internal affairs. If a dispute arose between member tribes, the league council could be asked to mediate the problem.

The position of sachem was hereditary in particular family lineages of each tribe. When a sachem died, his successor was chosen from among his kinsmen and was initially nominated by the matron of his lineage (with the approval of her kinswomen). She also had the prerogative of suggesting his recall if, later, he seemed to fail in his responsibilities. The influence of women in Iroquois society was an important part of the culture.

Organizational strength among the five tribes helped the Iroquois to spread their power far from their homeland. The acquisition of firearms from white men, plus the pressures and temptations of the fur trade influenced the Iroquois to subjugate neighboring Indians over a wide area. They brought many tribes under their domination, eventually took in the Tuscarora as the sixth nation of The League, and even adopted defeated enemies.

The League of The Iroquois became a mighty Indian power, especially after the British won the French and Indian War. Unfortunately, many Iroquois fought on the British side in the American Revolution. This was an unhappy choice for their future relations with the colonies that became the United States.

SEMINOLE

They lived in open, thatch-roofed dwellings raised on poles over the lowlands of The Everglades. They slipped over the wandering waterways in dugout canoes, silently spearing fish and departing. And no one, not even the United States Army, could completely dislodge the Seminole Indians from their Florida home.

The Seminoles developed in the 18th century from a diverse mixture of Creek and other Southeastern Indians who had entered Florida and mingled with earlier Indian inhabitants. The blending of these various groups (Hitchiti, Oconee, Apalachicola, Yuchi, Yamasee and others) formed the "Seminoles," which means those who had "broken off, run away."

During the emergence of the Seminoles, Florida was a remote frontier over which England, Spain and finally the United States struggled for control. Fugitive slaves settled there and became neighbors to the Indians. Additional Creeks fled into the area following the Creek War of 1813–14. Finally, during the course of the first, brief Seminole War, United States troops wrested control of Florida from the Spaniards, who formally relinquished their claims in 1819.

The Seminoles, who were now coming under the jurisdiction of the United States, had adapted well to their home. They hunted, farmed and fished in a generous land. Seminoles took deer and wild turkey, and planted melons, beans, corn and tobacco. These Indians dined on venison, hominy, corn cakes, honey and a jelly made from the root of China briar. Some lived in towns in houses of pole frames and timber, near buildings which stored potatoes, grains and other foods, amidst neatly swept yards and streets. Seminoles in differing environments preferred habitations which were basically unenclosed: raised platforms covered by peaked thatch roofs.

Their good life was reflected in zestful dress. Seminoles sported ostrich feathers worn in cloth turbans; shawls, buttoned leggings and silver crescent-shaped pendants worn about their necks. Many favored shirts and skirts with stripes of alternating bright colors and patterns.

White neighbors along the border had long viewed the Seminole lands as an irksome haven for runaway slaves. The homes of all Southeastern Indians were becoming more attractive to a growing influx of settlers. Owing to these and like pressures, the government decided to clear out the Indians and move them west of the Mississippi.

First the Seminoles were squeezed out of the good lands of northern and central Florida. Then they were told that they must cede all their lands and leave. A treaty required it, they were informed. The Seminoles did not go quietly.

From 1835 to 1842, the bitter second Seminole War raged across Florida. Tens of thousands of soldiers hounded the Indians. Seminoles raided and harassed the foe, then melted into the forests and swamps. One of their foremost leaders, Osceola, was tricked by a false flag of truce and captured in 1837. Still, bands of Seminoles fought on. Others were taken prisoner and shipped to what is now Oklahoma. An unknown number perished. Some 1,500 troops had been lost and a fortune squandered when the government finally gave up and allowed the last, undefeated Seminoles to remain hidden in The Everglades.

Some 3,000 Seminoles began their life anew in Oklahoma. Their kinsmen in Florida stayed in what was left of their homeland. They never surrendered. Their descendants are proudly there to this day.

CHIPPEWA

The Chippewa lived in a beautiful northern forest country laced with streams and rivers and dotted with lakes. They inhabited a region blessed with plentiful game and fish in Ontario, Canada and across Lake Superior into the upper peninsula of Michigan.

In this bountiful woodland the Chippewa hunted and fished. They crossed the vast, cold forests of winter on snowshoes and, in the warmer months, traveled the lakes and streams in light, swift birchbark canoes.

When summer came, families who had fanned out through the woods for the winter hunt would join together in a larger group, often at a favored fishing area. The Chippewa caught several kinds of fish in a number of ways, particularly sturgeon which they speared and whitefish which were netted. Along the rapids of the St. Mary's River at Sault Ste. Marie—which were rich with fish— Chippewa Indians rode the brisk currents in their canoes. A fisherman stood in the boat's bow wielding a long, forked pole with a net at the end. As the rapids carried the canoe along, the fisherman thrust his net into the swirling waters and hauled up several large whitefish until the canoe brimmed with the catch.

In some areas, berries and great amounts of wild rice were gathered. Some Chippewa planted corn in early summer, and collected maple sap in the spring to be made into maple sugar. But these activities, though significant, were secondary in importance to the hunting and fishing of the Chippewa.

Chippewa hunters used bows, arrows and spears, as well as traps and snares. Each large Chippewa band claimed a substantial hunting territory. In the autumn, a band separated into smaller family groups, each of which hunted over part of the shared grounds. The Chippewa searched for animals large and small—moose and mink, deer and rabbits, woodland caribou and beaver, otter, porcupine, fox and several more. Chippewa clans adopted animal names from bird, fish and land game. Members of each clan felt a special, perhaps religious, relationship with the animal from which the clan took its name. The bear was particularly respected and ceremonies were held when one had been killed.

The Chippewa needed a type of shelter which suited their wandering life. They dwelt in wigwams which were easily constructed and taken down. These oval, dome-shaped structures were built on a frame of saplings and covered with long, wide strips of birch bark which could be carried in rolls from one camp to another.

With the coming of the white man, change came to the world of the Chippewa, as it did to a greater or lesser degree to all Indians. Weapons, utensils and tools were obtained from white traders and began to supplement or replace native implements. Some Chippewa hunted and trapped for the fur trade as well as engaging in their traditional livelihoods. The tribe obtained firearms and moved into larger areas—even the Sioux in Minnesota felt the growing power of the Chippewa. These woodland Indians were fortunate in that their land was not as attractive to the white man as was other Indian land. Thus, even today, Chippewa Indians may be found living in some of their old areas, such as western Ontario.

SIOUX

The horse soldiers rode ever so proudly that summer's day in 1876. They followed their bold leader, eager for battle and glory. They knew the Indians would fall before their charge like wheat at the harvest. They would boast mightily of their deeds... but not one of the men who followed George Armstrong Custer lived to tell the tale of the Seventh Cavalry's fight with the Sioux.

The Sioux Indians, who, with the Cheyenne, won the great victory at the Little Bighorn River, are among the most famous of all Indians. Their life on the plains—the grand buffalo hunts and vast encampments of tepees—have largely defined our impression of American Indians. Yet this dramatic existence did not develop until late in their history—and it flowered all too briefly before it ended.

They did not call themselves "Sioux." That was a term used by their foes. "Dakota" is closer to the name they knew. And they were not one tribe, but several. They once inhabited a land of forest and lakes in upper Minnesota. They led a semi-settled life and hunted on foot. As their enemies to the northeast, the Chippewa, acquired guns from French traders, the Sioux moved toward the plains.

Santee Sioux (Sisseton, Wahpeton, Midewankton, and Wahpekute) remained in parts of Minnesota and nearby areas. The Yankton and Yanktonai crossed into the prairies of eastern South Dakota. The Tetons moved farthest west—and became the mightiest of all.

The Tetons were the people of Crazy Horse and Sitting Bull. They were among the warriors who destroyed the cavalry of Fetterman and Custer—and they were the followers of Red Cloud, the only Indians ever to win a war against United States troops. Their group names sing with the images of their wild and sacred Black Hills, the breathtaking high country of their Yellowstone and Powder River hunting lands—Miniconjou, Oglala, Brule, Hunkpapa, Sans Arc, Two Kettle and Sihasapa Sioux. They felt a kinship with their cherished land and they fought with a righteous fury to keep it.

Tetons were latecomers to the plains. They reached the Missouri River country well into the second half of the 18th century. But they adapted superbly. There, in a land of inspirational beauty, they became the Sioux of our history and legends. They collected horses—descendants of Spanish imports—and they encountered the seemingly endless herds of buffalo.

Buffalo gave them wealth. The Indians used practically every part of the animal. Meat was dried into jerky, or was finely pounded and mixed with dried berries and fat for pemmican. The hide was fashioned into clothing, containers, moccasins and materials to cover the conically-set tepee poles. Sinews were made into bowstrings and thread. Hoofs, bones and horns became tools and utensils. Even the "buffalo chips" were burned for fuel.

When winter left the plains, the scattered bands converged to form great tribal circles of tepees in preparation for the hunt. Horses pulled the Indian belongings on pole frameworks called "travois." Those possessions often included firearms, kettles, pots and decorative beads which the Sioux had received from white traders for skins and furs.

The search for buffalo, and the hunt itself, were highly disciplined, precise operations. The men skillfully guided their ponies to the ponderous beasts and struck with bow, arrow and lance.

They won respect on the hunt and in war. In battle, young men gained honor by "counting coup" against opponents in various specific ways of displaying courage. Recognition could be achieved by exploits other than killing.

But as this life bloomed to the fullest, the shadow of the encroaching white man fell over the plains. First the newcomers wanted to establish westward trails. Then they sought a path through Sioux hunting lands to Montana. Finally, they scrambled for gold in the Sioux' revered Black Hills.

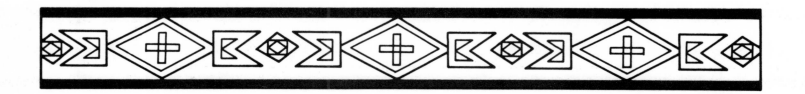

PAWNEE

Across the broad expanse of the Great Plains, migrations of American Indians surged and ebbed. Over the vast grasslands under enormous skies, tribes roved and settled. Among these tribes were the Pawnees, who occupied parts of Nebraska and adjacent areas.

The Skidis may have arrived there first. The Chauis, Kitkehahkis, and Pitahauerats came later. These four groups comprised the Pawnees.

They lived a semi-settled life of agriculture and hunting. The Pawnees erected villages—often large ones—of big, circular dwellings topped with sloped roofs with smoke holes at the peaks. The walls and roof of a lodge were covered with a thick earthen layer. The entrance projected outward at the end of an enclosed passageway. A few families lived in each one. Around these villages were the plots in which the Pawnees raised their crops. They felt a particular reverence for corn, which they usually crushed with a heavy pestle in a large wooden mortar. The Indians grew pumpkins, beans and squash, and collected edible roots and berries.

Pawnee hunters utilized traps and snares for small game. They displayed studied patience in stalking deer, elk, and buffalo.

Before they obtained horses, Pawnees silently encircled small groups of buffalo on foot. First one, then another of the Indians would cry out and frighten the beasts, making sure they kept the startled buffalo within their tightening ring. They moved in, shouting and waving robes in the air, until the panicked animals were stumbling about in fear and confusion. Then the hunters dropped the great creatures with arrows.

As Pawnees adopted the horse their lives changed significantly. The buffalo hunt became a grand tribal endeavor which took them from their settlements for several months each year. After the spring crops had been planted and the corn given its first hoeing, entire villages emptied as the Indians formed great columns to move west and south for the summer hunt. Men and women, crying children and barking dogs, hundreds of horses and mules all traveled toward the mighty buffalo herd. When the animals were located, the Indians formed a disciplined attack. Experienced hunters kept each man in his proper place. At just the right moment, they swooped down on the buffalo on swift ponies, firing arrows into their prey from several directions.

When the hunt was finished—and after they had gathered more horses by trading or raiding—Pawnees packed up their buffalo-skin lodges and returned to the villages for the happy time of harvest and festivals. The Indians then gathered in their crops and held wondrous "sleight-of-hand" performances which lasted twenty nights.

During these events, held in the great medicine lodges, Indians chanted, drummed and played music, and the "doctors" performed feats of magic that astounded all who watched. These mysteries were enacted inside a bare earth circle which was surrounded by spectators. Men disguised as elk were attacked with arrows that marvelously deflected and did no harm. Others were given terrible wounds that the doctors magically healed. Kernels of corn were planted and grew into stalks before people's eyes.

After this joyous harvest season passed, the Pawnees stored food in caches about their villages and departed for the autumn and winter hunt, to return in time to put in the spring crops.

This life came to an end. Their beloved Nebraska homeland was in the path of thousands of westward-bound settlers. They were harassed by enemies, particularly the Sioux. Finally, they were exiled into "Indian Territory" in Oklahoma, as were so many displaced tribes.

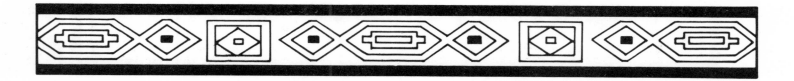

CHEROKEE

The Cherokee Indians of the Southeastern United States demonstrated substantial and successful adaptation to the white man's culture in the early 19th century. What happened to them showed how little such progress toward "civilization" mattered to whites who hungered for Indian land.

The Cherokees once lived in the region of the southern Allegheny Mountains—parts of Virginia, North and South Carolina, Tennessee and Georgia. White traders in the early 18th century found Cherokees living in settled towns. The main structure in such a town was a large, often circular, building of logs with an earthen roof where councils and other public business were conducted. In front of this imposing edifice was a town square used for dances, games and festivals. Nearby were a granary, gardens and the sturdy wooden homes of the Indians with adjacent poultry houses and orchards. Close at hand were the corn fields, and in the forests was game which the Cherokees vigorously hunted.

Warfare for the Cherokees, and other Southeastern Indians, was a way to gain honor and glory. It was more of a dangerous and deadly occupation than a policy of general conquest.

The Southeastern Indians occupied land that was increasingly attractive to whites. In the latter part of the 18th and first years of the 19th centuries, the Indians were persuaded to cede more and more territory to the young United States. Seeing the developing pattern, Cherokee leaders began to feel that their last hope for retaining their homelands lay in adopting the white man's ways.

Their progress was stunning. Schools were opened on Cherokee lands. A number of the Indians converted to Christianity. A Cherokee named Sequoyah developed a written alphabet for the Cherokee language in 1821 and many Cherokees learned to read and write. The Indians farmed, raised cattle, swine and sheep. They built sawmills and gristmills, and printed a newspaper, "Cherokee Phoenix," in both English and Cherokee. These Indians reorganized their tribal government. They created an elective legislature, a legal system, and divided their nation into judicial districts which came to be presided over by a Cherokee National Superior Court.

Other Southeastern Indians adapted to white ways in varying degrees. But whites wanted the land of the five civilized tribes (Cherokees, Creeks, Choctaws, Chickasaws and Seminoles). The state of Georgia was especially eager to see the Cherokees removed.

During the 1830's these five tribes were pressured to give up their lands and move west to "Indian Territory," in what is now the state of Oklahoma. The Cherokees were among the last to go and most of them went only when forced to leave.

In 1835, the government found a few Cherokees who were willing to sign a treaty relinquishing title to their lands. By far, the majority of Cherokees rejected this agreement and had no desire to move. Finally, in 1838, U.S. troops rounded up some 15,000 Cherokees, herded them into stockades, and, over the next several months, removed them hundreds of kilometers to a raw and alien frontier. This journey is known as "The Trail of Tears." Thousands died. A few hundred Cherokees hid in the caves and mountains of North Carolina for several years until they were finally allowed to remain. The rest of the Cherokee Nation was faced with the awesome task of rebuilding their world in a strange and faraway land.

BLACKFOOT

Winter wind swept down the northern plains from Canada. Inside a large tepee Blackfoot men in buffalo robes warmed themselves around a fire. With pleasure and contentment they shared a pipe and listened to the storyteller's tales of the summer's hunt. No one interrupted as he recalled daring horse-stealing raids and fondly recollected beloved legends. Their life was good, their land generous, and their people happy.

Blackfoot Indians once roamed over a vast territory to the east of the Rocky Mountains, from the Yellowstone River in Montana north into Canada to the Saskatchewan River country. Here, in a land of prairies and verdant river valleys, deep ravines and sharply rising buttes, the Blackfoot lived on nature's bounty. They feasted on deer, elk, antelope, wild mountain sheep—and uncounted thousands of buffalo.

The Blackfoot came to this area from Canadian timberlands to the Northeast. Three divisions (Blackfeet, Bloods and Pecunnies) composed the tribe and shared a common language and culture. They became outstanding plains Indians and adapted to the horse and buffalo life with great enthusiasm.

Horses were their wealth and war their sport. Blackfoot bands went long distances to collect these animals from their Indian foes. Young men gained honor by cleverly entering a hostile camp, running off the horses and by "counting coup" against enemies who opposed them. The bravest way to count coup was to boldly confront a worthy enemy and strike him with the hand or a hand-held weapon. This expressed personal valor and disdain for danger. Such courageous acts against adversaries often brought a warrior more fame than did killing.

Raiding and hunting kept the Blackfoot in splendid physical condition. In summer or winter, men usually began their day by bathing in rivers near their camps. Their strength and endurance was more than equal to the strenuous life. Men sought to join various age-graded warrior societies which were responsible for guarding encampments, protecting the bands as they moved to new hunting grounds and presenting certain dances and ceremonies. Their ceremonial attire was often stunning, sometimes decorated with ermine fur or eagle feathers.

At times, men went off alone to some wild and dangerous spot to fast and pray. In this way a Blackfoot hoped to be granted a vision, or "medicine dream," which would bring him good fortune. Through rigorous supplication, a man might be visited by a spirit—often in animal form—which would counsel him and teach him a special way to win glory. It was an awesome personal event.

Women were hard-working and held vital responsibilities. They made camp, did much of the butchering during the hunt, tanned hides, prepared fur robes and dried great quantities of meat. With this they made pemmican, which was finely pounded meat mixed with bone marrow and dried berries, then stored in large hides. (A second grade of pemmican was composed of pounded dried meat and melted animal tallow.) The woman who set up the medicine lodge was especially respected and a women's society held sacred duties for the Sun Dance, the most precious of Blackfoot ceremonies.

The Blackfoot had no reason to want their world changed. But in the 19th century white traders and trappers brought contagious diseases which the Blackfoot had never known. A great many died. Then the commercial hunters arrived, shot the buffalo for the hides and let the meat rot on the prairie. They killed until hardly any animals were left. Soon the cherished old ways were gone. The once abundant Blackfoot life became a struggle for survival.

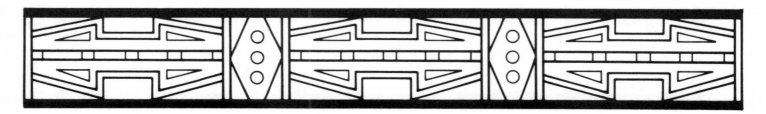

NEZ PERCE

Their home was a land of high mountain meadows and wild flowers, cool streams, sheltered valleys and shaded evergreen forests. On this bountiful Northwestern plateau, the Nez Perce Indians lived in peace and raised beautiful horses. They wanted to preserve the generous earth for their children, as their people had for hundreds of years.

But the white man's government told them to leave the green hillsides that had heard the songs of their mothers. And before their ordeal was over, some of these Indians had led the U.S. Cavalry on a 2167 kilometer (1300-mile) chase and had come within a day's ride of escaping into Canada.

Nez Perce gained fame as breeders of magnificent Appaloosas. But for most of their long history they had no horses. They lived where the states of Washington, Oregon and Idaho now meet, in the country of the Clearwater, Salmon and Snake Rivers. Originally dwelling in fishing villages along rivers, they built large, multi-family lodges of timbers topped with grass and cattail mats. Salmon was the mainstay of their diet. Nez Perce hunted elk, deer, bear and mountain sheep, and gathered berries and edible roots from the meadows.

Spanish invaders introduced horses into the New World in the 16th century, but it was a long time after that before Indians had them in large numbers. The Nez Perce acquired horses perhaps as early as the end of the 17th century. First the new creatures were wonderful luxuries. Then the Indians found that their well-watered plateaus and secure valleys were almost perfect horse country.

These Indians developed their horse herds with great care. They selectively bred their animals by gelding or trading away inferior specimens and importing superior breeding stock. This produced well-built, strong horses that were highly prized. The tribe especially favored the colorful, spotted Appaloosas, an ancient breed which the Nez Perce diligently perfected.

They adapted to the new mobility of the horse. Bands of Nez Perce crossed the Rocky Mountains and met, traded with and fought other Indians on the high, northern plains. They hunted buffalo and lived in skin-covered tepees. They adopted the eagle-feather headdress, horse accessories, games and customs from their new acquaintances. Even the many Nez Perce who remained in their traditional homelands could not help but be affected.

The white man brought more changes. The Lewis and Clark expedition was aided by the Nez Perce in 1805–06. After that positive encounter, the Indians endeavored to be friendly to whites for decades. Their good will was not appreciated. Gold and land-hungry whites swarmed over their domain. In 1855 and 1863 treaties slashed away huge portions from the Indians' territories until the Nez Perce were left with only a reservation on the Clearwater River in Idaho.

Many of these Indians did not sign away their lands. Among them was a man of great eloquence and dignity—Chief Joseph. With a large, peaceful band of Nez Perce, thousands of horses and many cattle, Joseph remained in the beautiful Wallowa River valley in Washington and Oregon. In 1877 he was given a month's notice to move to the reservation.

He tried to comply with the abrupt deadline, but brutal acts by men of both races forced Joseph and several hundred Indians—the majority of whom were women and children—to flee eastward. They were pursued and repeatedly attacked by outnumbering U.S. troops. The Indians fought off and eluded their hunters time and again. For several months Joseph and other great warriors led the Indians along 2167 kilometers of rugged mountains and tangled woods, through Idaho, Wyoming and into Montana, where they were finally trapped a scant 50 kilometers (30 miles) from the Canadian border.

Joseph surrendered and lived out his life in exile. He was a man of great leadership and compassion for his people. Chief Joseph's surrender speech is one of the most famous in Indian literature. It concludes as follows: "I want to have time to look for my children and see how many of them I can find. Maybe I shall find them among the dead. Hear me, my chiefs. I am tired. My heart is sick and sad. From where the sun now stands I will fight no more forever."

HAIDA

The Haida shared in one of the richest and most colorful of North American Indian cultures. Haida and similar Indians of the Northwest Pacific Coast (Kwakiutl, Nootka, Tsimshian, Tlingit and several other groups) were favored by both climate and an abundant natural food supply. In this hospitable environment, their creativity flourished.

British Columbia's Queen Charlotte Islands and the southern part of Alaska's Prince of Wales Island was the home of the Haida. Comparable bands of Indians inhabited the narrow coastal areas and many islands from the Alaska panhandle along the Canadian coast into the Northwest United States. Here the warm waters of the Japanese Current give rise to a weather system graced with much rainfall and moderate temperatures with only slight seasonal variation.

Into the rivers and streams of the area enormous numbers of salmon came to spawn. Herring, smelt and cod were plentiful as were clams, mussels and other mollusks. Sea mammals such as seal and otter provided good hunting. The land was alive with bear, deer, elk and beaver.

The coastal Indians harvested, preserved and stored great amounts of fish (especially salmon) and thus had substantial time to develop strong traditions in art and culture. The two most famous of these are distinctive woodcarving and the great ceremony called the potlatch.

Haida woodworkers are renowned for their totem poles. Large tree trunks (often red cedar) were carved with representations of ancient supernatural beings which held ancestral significance for the kinsmen erecting the pole. Memorable family history was also depicted. The totemic figures sometimes took the form of stylized eagles, ravens, whales or bears. Such poles often rose high above the gabled roof in front of the large, rectangular wooden house of the Haida. Totem poles also served as memorials to past chiefs. Commemorative symbols of a family's heritage were also carved into boxes, huge seaworthy canoes, posts and beams of houses and a variety of other objects.

The importance of age-old family rights and lore expressed in the totem poles flowered magnificently in the potlatch.

The potlatch was a crucial ritual which reinforced the honored traditions of the group and the status of each member. A chief could give a potlatch for a number of reasons. One of these was to formally proclaim an heir and legitimize the heir's right to all honors due him. The chief's kin gathered with him, often in a large house. All contributed to the store of wealth which would be given away at the potlatch. A neighboring group arrived as guests and to this combined assembly, the host chief explained how his rights and privileges had come down through his family from ancient times. He detailed his heir's rights to family crests, titles and possessions. The guests witnessed and acclaimed these rights.

Then, all guests were given gifts appropriate to their individual rank. Great collections of wealth—copper plates, blankets, furs—were given away. As the amount of gifts increased, the glory of the giver and his family grew. Potlatches sometimes included feasting and ceremonial dancing, often with elaborately carved masks. Details of potlatches differed among the Northwest Coast Indians, but the essentials of form and purpose were shared.

Though their lives and culture have significantly changed, many Northwest Coast Indians still live in some of their traditional homelands continuing their time-honored arts.

POMO

Some distance north of San Francisco Bay lies a coastal region of foggy, windswept bluffs broken by rivers and creeks which flow from the interior. Farther inland are sunny ridges and the small, enclosed valleys of the Russian River. Eastward still in this hilly country is the spacious expanse of Clear Lake. This was the land of the Pomo Indians, famous for their superb basket-making artistry.

Pomo occupied territory from below Russian River in the south to just above the Noyo River northward, and inland to the Clear Lake region. They ate a variety of wild foods. The Coastal Pomo, who inhabited level, sheltered areas on the creek and river mouths, took salmon which annually swam upstream to spawn, as well as surf fish, abalone, mussels and sometimes sea lions. The Indians who dwelled in the interior regions fished, hunted small game and deer, and gathered a variety of bulb plants.

Acorns were a staple of the Pomo diet, as with many California Indians. Pomo ground the acorns into meal. They poured water through the meal to leach out the unpleasant tasting tannic acid. The meal was boiled with hot stones in baskets or perhaps mixed with red, ferruginous earth and baked in an earth oven. Acorns could be naturally leached by storing them in damp grounds near lakes, streams and springs. As time passed, the bitter taste left and the acorns became tasty snacks for the Indians to dig up when they returned.

The Pomo adapted their houses to available materials. The Coastal Pomo (and those who lived in a nearby area of heavy timber) arranged redwood bark slabs into a conical shaped structure. Russian River Pomo used a thatched grass covering over a circular or rectangular framework of poles. The Pomo of the Clear Lake region preferred a thatch of tule rushes rather than grass for their house-covering.

Clear Lake Pomo Indians built light canoes of bundled tule rushes (which were called *balsas* in Spanish). The coastal dwellers constructed log rafts to traverse short distances—to reach offshore sea lion rocks, for instance.

The Pomo were famous for the creativity expressed in their shell money and beautiful baskets. Their money was made from pieces of clamshell which were ground round, bored, strung and polished. Another highly regarded type were the finger-length cylindrical beads made from magnesite, which was carefully shaped, polished and baked. The heat brought out lustrous shades of color.

The Pomo developed basket-making into a true art. Even everyday cooking and storage baskets were well-made and ornamented. In addition to practical uses, they served as hats, toys, gifts and treasures. Cherished ones were destroyed to honor and mourn the dead.

Pomo employed a variety of twine, coil and even wickerwork techniques. They used several materials: willow, root of sedge and digger pine. The bark of redbud was used for red patterns and bulrush root was dyed for black.

Basket decoration was often stunning. Black, wavy quail plumes and scarlet feathers from woodpeckers' crowns were used to good effect. The exterior of some baskets were masses of feathers. Beads were also employed. Designs were arranged in horizontal, diagonal, vertical, crossing, radiated or banded patterns. The Pomo never completely encircled a basket with a banded design, however. A break was always left in a band, it is said, to insure that the maker would not go blind. Sometimes an initial design was placed at the start of a basket for religious reasons.

Pomo Indians had early contact with Russian settlers on the California coast at Fort Ross, with whom they enjoyed better relations than did nearby Indians with Spaniards. In modern days, Pomo have worked at ranching, fishing, and timber activities in their old lands. A few still preserve the Pomo traditions of basketry.

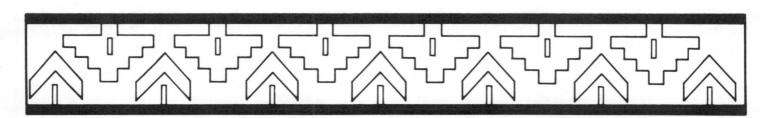

RIO GRAND
PUEBLOS

Indians of the Rio Grande Pueblos spoke different languages and lived in independent villages. Though each group was distinct, all shared important cultural similarities.

The art of these New Mexico Indians reflects their varied yet comparable heritages. Different pueblos maintain individual styles of brilliantly colored pottery design, yet employ the same fundamental techniques.

Pueblo Indians were settled agriculturalists, as were the Hopi and Zuni. But unlike those desert people, the Rio Grande Indians irrigated their fields with river water and built their pueblos primarily of adobe, rather than of stone.

River Pueblos lie along the Rio Grande and adjacent streams from Isleta and Sandia Pueblos in the south to Picuris and Taos in the north. Between these geographic points, two major language groups—Tanoan and Keresan—were spoken in a number of variations. For instance, at Jemez Pueblo the people spoke Towa, a Tanoan language, while further down the Jemez Creek at Zia, a Keresan dialect prevailed.

Yet a common bond held both desert and river Pueblos together. The impressive organization and cultural integration of Pueblo Indian societies was founded upon religious beliefs and ceremonies. The Indians strove to order their lives properly and to offer their prayers correctly so the gods would grant rain, bountiful crops and happiness to the people. There were, and are, significant differences in emphasis and form among the Pueblo peoples—but in broad outline, their several worlds are one.

Their cultural strengths have seen them through great adversity. Spanish colonists arrived in 1598, determined to subjugate the old Pueblo societies. The newcomers tried to alter many aspects of Indian life—especially the vital religious practices. Spanish churches were imposed on the Indians and many native ceremonies were forbidden. In 1680, the Pueblo peoples rose up and furiously drove the Spaniards out. After twelve years, the invaders finally returned with their cross and their guns. But even today, aspects of the original faiths of the Pueblo Indians endure.

Pottery-making skills of some of the river Pueblo Indians have also survived. Though their craftsmanship in this field had markedly declined under the pressures of cultural change, the art has undergone a positive revival in this century. The Pueblos of Acoma, Zia, Santa Clara, San Ildefonso, Santo Domingo, Cochiti and San Juan are particularly noted for their work.

The Indians fashion pottery in a traditional manner. They use clay tempered with sand and smoothed with water. A base of this material is prepared and, without using a potters' wheel, successive layers of rolled clay are coiled on and shaped by hand. The piece is then dried and often a "slip" (clay highly thinned with water) is applied and then polished with a smooth stone. Indian pottery is painted and decorated before it is fired. Colors are made from mineral earths and other natural sources. Brushes are developed from the fibers of chewed yucca leaves.

When a number of pieces are ready to be fired, they are arranged upside down on a grate among a bed of hot coals. The vessels are sheltered by large shards of broken pottery. Fire is built around the pots as fuel is stacked over them in a dome of glowing materials which burn on the inside.

Each Pueblo maintains its own patterns and designs. Symbols used include serpents and birds, rain and water figures, geometric arrangements, sky and cloud forms. The styles of design and the art of pottery-making itself are important elements in an Indian culture which, though changed, is very much alive.

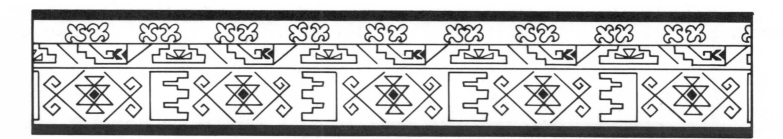

ZUNI

In the fine craftsmanship of their turquoise and silver jewelry, in the fabulous designs of their dance masks and in their wealth of ceremonial observances, the Zuni Indians have displayed a creative spirit which has brought great beauty to their desert home.

The Zuni now occupy an area along the Zuni River, south of Gallup, New Mexico. Their old home was a terraced, stone and adobe pueblo on a hill overlooking the river. Originally they lived primarily by agriculture, raising corn, beans, squash and chiles. During the last hundred years, or so, Zuni Indians developed skills as jewelry-makers—and are now famous for this work.

Zuni use a variety of jewelry designs—deer, butterflies, eagles, dance figures in flat relief and more—in which turquoise stones are individually set or arranged in mosaics. Different colors of stone, shell and coral pieces, delicately elaborate designs and silverwire trim often distinguish Zuni creations. Jewelry-making has joined agriculture as their important economic activities.

The artistry expressed by the jewelry-makers was traditionally found in the fertile imagery of the abundant religious dances and ceremonials of the Zuni. Kiva groups, priesthoods, fraternities and medicine societies played important roles in preserving sacred traditions and observances. For it was through proper attention to ritual and prayer that rain, fertility and a joyful life were granted by the gods.

Religious dances were not diversions from a rigorous life, but a highly important unifying element in the Zuni harmony with life. Dances were held often throughout the year, except during the crucial planting and harvest seasons.

Masks became a vital element in these dances. The Zuni were renowned for the skill in construction, imagination in design and the sheer variety of their masks. They were bizarre, often grotesque creations, symbolically painted and, at times, impressively large. The masks used for the Shalako festival after the harvest were as much as three meters (nine feet) high and enclosed the men who danced within them.

The Zuni sun priest set the dates for the dances. In the summer, rain dances were held. In winter, members of the Wood Fraternity—men and women—performed the dances of the sword swallowers. With great dexterity they combined dancing with swallowing red-colored swords made of juniper and decorated with feathers. Their rites lasted for several days. The medicinal powers of the Wood Fraternity were said to have been most useful for treating sore throats.

The climax of the year was the Shalako ceremonial, held in November or December. This was a symbolic representation of the Zuni's creation and migration to their homeland. Dancers completely enveloped in huge, awe-inspiring masks personified the Shalako, divine messengers from the rain gods who devoted prayers to the happiness and fruitful life of the Zuni.

Preparations for this festival went on throughout the year. Participants honored special rites to prepare themselves for their roles. As the great time approached, special houses built for the Shalako were decorated, great amounts of bread baked and meals readied. Finally a masked, nude youth painted black with red, yellow, blue and white spots, representing the fire-god, appeared carrying a burning cedar brand. He was followed by a Council of Gods and finally, by the six Shalako. These figures were striking, enormous masks with eagle-feather headdresses, turquoise faces with rolling, bulging eyes, clacking beaks, and accents of long black hair and ravens' feathers. These marvels were received in their houses where they danced through the night. Truly, the gods seemed to be among their people.

The Zuni have preserved much of their heritage to this day. Many of their dances survive.

APACHE

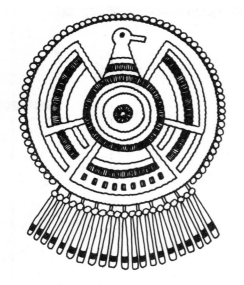

In the harsh desert and ragged mountains of the American Southwest, some men's eyes saw only a wasteland. But to the Apache Indians, this seemingly unfriendly environment was dotted with wild foods and useful materials. In a demanding, dangerous terrain, Apaches displayed great strength, resourcefulness and more than enough ability to adapt and even to thrive.

Apaches were a wandering people and their long journey into the Southwest is an ancient, indistinct saga. In the last few centuries they ranged from northern Mexico to southern Colorado, from areas of the Great Plains to Arizona and New Mexico. They traveled in many separate divisions in differing habitats. Some adopted elements of plains culture, others were influenced by pueblo peoples and the Navajo (to whom they were related). Through many years of contact with Spaniards, Mexicans and White Americans they remained fiercely independent and gloriously free—for as long as they possibly could.

They roamed in many bands led by trusted individuals. Eastern Apaches were the Jicarilla, Mescalero, Chiricahua and Lipan divisions. Their western kinsmen were the White Mountain, Cibecue, San Carlos and Tonto tribes. Some, like the plains-dwelling Jicarilla, lived in tepees and hunted buffalo. Others, including the Chiricahuas of the southern mountains, built "wickiups" of leafy branches and grass arranged over a dome-shaped frame. Apaches found deer and wild berries in forested mountain valleys, and agave plants, yucca fruits and mesquite beans on the arid lands. They grew gardens where they could and raided for horses and sheep when they chose.

Their land and life demanded much and the Indians responded with imagination and creativity. Apaches designed handsome beadwork patterns to enhance buckskin garments, and developed a range of practical, decorative basketry, including large burden carriers, watertight canteens, even sunshades on cradle boards.

Beneath the tough exterior of the mescal plant they found its juicy heart. From cooked mescal, cactus fruit or corn, Apaches fermented drinks called "tulibai." They derived nourishment from the inner bark of yellow pine trees, cattail and tumbleweed roots as well as occasional rattlesnakes.

Raiding was their business and they were thorough professionals. Apaches rigorously prepared for the stress of this activity and developed ways to conceal themselves that frustrated pursuers, who shrunk at the prospect of following Indians into the mountain strongholds.

Apaches were stern foes to those who coveted their lands. Tales and myths of savage Apaches were fostered by those who had great crimes of their own to hide. An inconsistent and often shameful government policy drove angry Apache bands to their ancient mountain refuges time and again. Sadly, it is the exploits of Geronimo that people remember, rather than the many reasons that set him on his desperate path.

But today, in an expression of their endurance and courage, Apaches have built positive, constructive lives. Some have become stock raisers, foresters, successful conservationists and administrators. While they share the problems of rapid cultural change and adjustment which face many Indians, they have overcome hardships before. That is their heritage.

HOPI

They called themselves "The Peaceful Ones." In their dry, demanding land, the Hopi Indians developed a life rich in art and ceremony, an imaginative culture which flowered despite the desert's harshness.

Hopi still live on three high mesas in northeastern Arizona where their people have been for a very long time. Over the centuries they built solid pueblo villages, learned to find hidden water that nourished their crops, and danced in stunning masks to send prayers to the gods.

Buildings in a traditional Hopi village were large edifices of stone plastered with adobe, sometimes three stories high. Each level was set back about a room's width from the front of the one below. The structures were arranged against one another. The ground floors were usually for storage and originally were entered from above. Upper floors were reached by removable ladders. All in all, it was a secure arrangement.

In their agricultural life, the Hopi demonstrated the adaptability of American Indians. In the desert surrounding their homes they planted in low areas beneath which water accumulated, or over the paths of underground streams. Hopi spaced corn hills several feet apart and placed a number of seeds in each one with the aid of a long digging stick. Corn came up in bushy clumps in which the ears were sheltered under many leaves. They also raised squash, beans, tobacco, and even cotton. Hopi supplemented their diet with rabbits and other game.

Hopi artistry was displayed in basket-making and pottery, in patterned sashes and blankets of woven cotton, and in the great variety of carved, imaginative kachina dolls.

These dolls were part of the detailed religious and ceremonial life of the Hopi. Ceremonies were held throughout the year, carefully preserved and handed down through the generations. Many took place in structures called kivas. (Hopi kivas were circular and built with only the roof above ground level.) Other, more public dances, were held in open squares. Through these events, the Hopi sought to secure the favor of the gods who would provide rain and the renewal of all life.

During about half the year, Hopi ceremonies featured special costumed and masked dancers. These men represented the many kachinas, supernatural spirits who in some way might intercede between man and the deities. The highly stylized masks were decorated with painted symbols, headdresses of feathers or hair, beaks, horns, wings and other symbolic features. When the dancers performed, the spirits which they represented were felt to be present as well.

The kachina dancers filed to one side of the plaza, keeping time with rattles on their legs and in their hands, and singing. They repeated their actions on other sides of the square and sometimes gave presents to the children before retiring. During the intervals before the dancers reappeared, antic clowns painted in black and white stripes entertained, and sometimes satirized, the spectators.

Kachina spirits were also represented in dolls which Hopi men carved from cottonwood. These dolls were careful reproductions of the costumes and masks of the dancers. Children were not supposed to view the dolls as toys, but as a means to learn to recognize the various kachinas and appreciate their significance. Dolls had individual names—Deer Kachina, Homedance Maiden, Black Ogre, Mudhead Clown, Prickly Pear Kachina, and many more. Each doll was delicately formed and distinctly different in appearance from the others.

Today, the Hopi live in their old homeland. They have adapted and changed, but also have preserved much of their treasured culture—including the wonderful dolls.

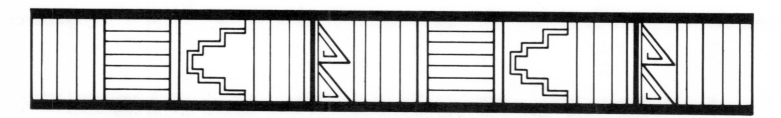

NAVAJO

A little over one hundred years ago, the Navajo Indians were in exile at a stark desert encampment in New Mexico. With all their hearts, they longed for home, hundreds of miles to the west. Only there, in "Dinetah," could the Navajo live in happiness—for it was more than their land. It was part of them. It was sacred.

At last the U.S. government let them return. Since that bitter time, the Navajo has become the largest Indian tribe in the United States. They have retained their culture and identity on the special earth which is as a mother to them.

The Navajo—or "Dineh," The People—live on or near a 40,000 sq. km. (25,000 sq. mile) reservation in northeastern Arizona, northwestern New Mexico and southern Utah. For centuries this territory of mesas and buttes, canyons and pine-forested mountains has been their special place. Many of the outstanding physical features of the terrain are shrines to them. The land, everything in it, the sky above and the Navajo themselves are one in an ancient harmony. Thus their lives, world and religion are one and the same—in a way that only they can truly understand.

An appreciation of Navajo philosophy may lead to a realization of why they strenuously opposed white men's efforts to change their beliefs and place of residence. Yet the Navajo have been far from inflexible. They borrowed cultural elements (particularly from the Pueblo Indians, who may have given them upright loom weaving and some ceremonies) but adapted these acquisitions into distinctly Navajo forms.

From the Spaniards they obtained sheep and horses—and their lives were altered. Originally hunters and agriculturalists, the Navajo became stock raisers. They still planted corn and other crops—even fruit orchards and melons where the land permitted—but the growing herds of animals brought them a new bounty and allowed a flowering of Navajo culture.

When these Indians maintained the proper relations with the natural and supernatural world, all was well. But if a Navajo caused an imbalance, illness or distress might result. Curative ceremonies were held to restore the afflicted person to harmony with the universe. The ceremonies were specific and complex, requiring songs, dances and sand paintings. The sand paintings were stylized, symbolic representations of Navajo legends which were created on an unwound buckskin on the floor of a ceremonial structure. The artists used colored sands and other natural elements to prepare an elaborate and beautiful design—which would then be destroyed in the course of the ceremony.

Navajo also displayed philosophical views in the design of homes. Their hogans, which were rounded dwellings of pole-frames covered with earth, always had entrances facing east to welcome the morning sun. And if someone died in a hogan, it was burned. (Some hogans came to be built of logs, or stone with mud in a six-sided pattern.)

The Navajo world was brutally disrupted by Spaniards, Mexicans and Americans. The sad history of the invaders climaxed (1863–64) when U.S. troops swept through the Navajo land, burning hogans, killing sheep, destroying crops and giving the Indians a choice between starving and moving. Many, but not all, of the Navajo were taken on "The Long Walk" to Fort Sumner in New Mexico. It was a barren place where life was miserable. After four grievous years, they were allowed to resettle on a portion of "Dinetah." It seemed the white man didn't want their land after all.

In the years following, the Navajo increased the size of their reservations significantly. They began to trade in their beautiful woven rugs and blankets, and finely crafted silver jewelry.

Navajo population has risen to over 125,000. The People are finding new ways to adjust to a white man's world, while carefully preserving the essential characteristics of the Navajo way.

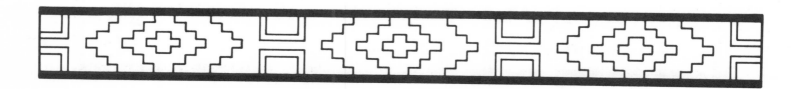

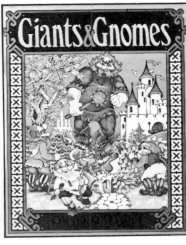